The Forever Parade

poems by

Drew Attana

Finishing Line Press
Georgetown, Kentucky

The Forever Parade

Copyright © 2016 by Drew Attana
ISBN 978-1-63534-039-6 First Edition
All rights reserved under International and Pan-American Copyright Conventions.
No part of this book may be reproduced in any manner whatsoever without written permission from the publisher, except in the case of brief quotations embodied in critical articles and reviews.

ACKNOWLEDGMENTS

"How to Touch a Woman" and "Bar Fight" first appeared in *Apeiron Review*
"Parallel Parking" first appeared in *Phoebe Literary Journal*
"Cheap Cigarettes," and "The Content is Irrelevant" first appeared in *Common Ground Review*
"That Night We Drove to the Gulf After the Bar Closed" first appeared in *West Trade Review*
"Security Deposit" first appeared in Phoebe Literary Journal
"Yeller Yeller" and "Thief" first appeared in *Merrimack Review*
"Gunbearer" first appeared in *Yellow Chair Review*,
"Funky Tucks," "This is a Felony," and "That Street with All the Food Carts" first appeared in *Eunoia Review*
"Lockdown" first appeared in *Drunk Monkeys Magazine*
"Time to Buzz the Tower, Goose," and "Boys Will Be Boys" first appeared in *Holy Shit Literary Journal*
"Navigating the Cultural Practices of Suburban Wisconsinites" first appeared in *Shark Reef*

Publisher: Leah Maines

Editor: Christen Kincaid

Cover Art: Susan David

Author Photo: Susan David

Cover Design: Elizabeth Maines

Printed in the USA on acid-free paper.
Order online: www.finishinglinepress.com
       also available on amazon.com

Author inquiries and mail orders:
Finishing Line Press
P. O. Box 1626
Georgetown, Kentucky 40324
U. S. A.

Table of Contents

How to Touch a Woman 1

Bar Fight 2

Parallel Parking 3

That Night We Drove to the Gulf after the Bar Closed 4

Thief 5

Funky Tucks 6

Yeller Yeller 7

This is a Felony 8

Navigating the Cultural Practices of Suburban
    Wisconsinites 9

Spit Shine 10

Cheap Cigarettes 11

The Content is Irrelevant 12

Security Deposit 13

Lockdown 14

Time to Buzz the Tower, Goose 16

Gunbearer 17

Boys Will Be Boys 18

That Street with All the Food Carts 19

*For Kay Cash
and all those times she let me sneak over
and watch reruns of Columbo*

How to Touch a Woman

Paperback romances
and those flashy,
photoshopped magazines
lining grocery store checkout lines
tell me that sharing her bed,
her eager body,
that exploring the depth
of her fantasies
is the height of intimacy,
yet they say nothing
of making sure the lights
are separate from the darks,
of choosing Black Cherry wood stain
for the shelves you built together,
or the necessity of your hand
placed not in strategic erogenous zones,
but on the small of her back,
the pressure keeping her stable
as she reads for her grandmother,
for her family,
while her black heels sink
inch by inch,
into the soft mud
of an Oshkosh graveyard.

Bar Fight

I had a dog who used to scratch at his eyes
when the pollen was high, so much that
he would look like he'd come out the loser
in a bar fight. I see him most days, in piles

of dirty laundry or under the crumpled thrust
of hand-me-down comforters. Spread out
like a bathmat on the cool tiles. At a knock
on the front door, I still hear the clatter of nails,

long past the need for clipping, and the stern
tone of his bark, a marriage of menace
and curiosity, though all that echoes on wood
floors and poster-filled walls is the snap, crackle

and pop of vinyl, the swirling notes of Elton's
baby grand as he teases out some fondness from
the dead-eye of yesterday—before the splitting
of bank accounts, the division of yet unopened

wedding gifts, before my first w-a-l-k down
the sharp diagonal of Foster Road, into the park
without the urgency of the frayed, red leash pulled
taut or even thought of carrying his leash at all.

Parallel Parking

When she pulled over, I wonder
if she bothered to kill the engine.

I wonder if she left the radio on,
tuned to some local station buzzing
with the same tracks she'd played
in her basement room, while thumbing
through an old Penthouse, spreading
out the centerfold to show me everything
I'd ever need to know about the world.

I wonder if she'd bought the bag
on the same block where they found her,
from a friend of a friend of a friend,
and if she did, I hope it was as black
as her wardrobe during those long weeks
after Kurt's shotgun show in ninety-four.

When she let go of the wheel, I wonder
if she bothered to take the spike out.

I wonder if she hid everything, spoon
and rubber, under the seat, or left it all
on the dash, free to absorb the daylight,
the understanding of the neighborhood
kids, same age as her own, stumbling
by her window and learning everything
they'd ever need to know about the world.

I wonder if she had somewhere to be
or just leaving to run a few errands,
a long list to finish after one quick stop,
and if she was, I hope she tucked it away,
deep enough that her family wouldn't
find it and pick up where she left off.

That Night We Drove to the Gulf After the Bar Closed

a year ago, we ran away
to the end of our world,
an hour's drive to where
the black water of the Gulf

scratched against sleeping
boats and the lonely pier—
its beaten wood groaning
beneath the weight of us,

our dancing and drive-thru
daiquiris and fruitless star
gazing through the winter
coat of fog, close enough

above us that we could
almost reach up and touch
the dream of what we'd left
behind—old friends, lovers,

signposts of a life different
than what we'd expected,
and we stayed like that
until our drinks melted

and our voices grew hoarse;
until Cajun fisherman, rising
with the sun, slung lines
through the scattering haze

sending us Northerners
packing, back to the safety
of the dented Corolla
that would take us home

to another morning of cold
sheets and phone calls back
home and the impossibility
of what will come next.

Thief

I used to steal
make-up from drug stores
and fistfuls of classic
cinema from now
bankrupt rental chains.
I've walked right
out of a loading dock
carrying one corner
of a pool table,
and pushed through
the emergency exit
with a nose
of a grocery cart,
its rickety wheels
groaning with liquid cargo.
I've raided roommate's music
collections and closets,
and I've pocketed loose
change from party countertops.
I've stolen the right words,
and lied about car accidents,
fist fights, and every
little insignificance
of my past.
I've convinced friends
and lovers
that I really am the man
I keep saying I am,
and in the same breath
I've stolen
that earnest hush from
the bathroom mirror
when I tell myself,
one goddamn day,
I will be.

Funky Tucks

Walking home from the parades I crunch
and smash the leftover revelry beneath my feet:
beads and pizza slices and strewn feathers
without station, or heritage
thrown to the same grasping fingers.

Before the firetruck rolled through, all polished,
shined like the freshest pair of sneaks, the floats
disseminated strand after strand to us.
All walks, shouting and cheering and grabbing.
A football to a young boy, panties to the girl
and we heard music, from this porch and that,
from white and from black.

Swinging from my neck are the spoils,
what I fought and clawed for, the heft
of long, outstretched arms and the desire to become.

Resting over them, a purple glossy chain
holding a pendant to my belly, with the likeness
of a man: dreadlocks and black skin and gold teeth.
> The text says, "Funky Tucks," and I have no idea
> what this means, or who he is, but I know his likeness
> was thrown to me, to my hand.

The sound of firetruck's horn signals an end, the end
to Professor Longhair, sparkled masks, and painted faces,
to the forever parade.
We diverged, separated to our porches, forgetting
the beating drums, and linked arms.

The collective howl.

The steel-teethed sweepers will leave their garages after dusk,
and in the morning,
the streets will be clear again.

Yeller Yeller

I see him still, his wild eyes
flushed like brake lights.
The traffic had parted, swerving
around him as he limped along

parallel yellow lines leading
the asphalt path to the sea.
He paused to gnaw at himself
then spin, round and round,

like a top, or an anxious mind.
As I got out to help, he rushed
at me, all foam and daze,
his golden fur matted, shellacked

from previous hits, but rather
than attack, he brushed by my leg,
—collar jingling, singing a life
line home, his bent tail wagging

out of habit or memory—and ran
head first into the hard plastic
bumper of a slowing Mustang,
smoke and rubber tracks left

behind in the concrete wake.
But he wasn't done yet:
On his feet with a shake and snort,
he took off, running as if he'd just

discovered legs, off the highway
through the weeds and brush,
aimed at the parting tree line
and the great Ocean beyond.

This is a Felony

On my mother's side, the men worked
the train lines, repairing ties and running
off hoppers with their cinematic knapsacks
and sloshing glass bottles of bathtub spirits.

My grandfather brought cars together,
getting in close between and coupling
gnarled steel knuckles by hand. A long haul
going West, carrying milk or Lucky Strikes,

took his fingers before leaving the yard.
They're still running, these freighters
these thieves, crisscrossing paths
like active circuitry, long blasts of the air

Horns like passing salutes, and while we busy
ourselves with texts and status updates
and the knuckled grip of the armrests
before the seatbelt light switches off,

the trains keep on as they have, choking
and puffing down the way, scaring
children off and waking neighborhoods
and flattening the occasional penny

or rusted Ford stalled across the tracks.
My first time in a train yard, I wasn't working.
I held paint cans and a grudge and I went
after the closest engine, only getting half

my name out before a friend stopped me,
saying we never write on those—not ever.
These fuckers work for us, he told me,
taking little pieces of us everywhere.

Navigating the Cultural Practices of Suburban Wisconsinites

I learned to listen for the low squeak
of cheese curds between my teeth,

that noise matching the satisfaction
of new flavor and even newer family,

and you and I sat somewhere inside
the expanse of porch and wilderness

watching locally packed bratwursts
sizzle and burst on the grill, letting

your mom talk about men and women
and about what she needed to do next

until both night and he came home—
her man—smelling of dirt and smoke,

and we watched him crack a High Life,
then lug a box of illegal fireworks up

from the basement and insist we all aim
Roman Candles at the crawling tree-line,

the edge of this world guarded by strings
of bird houses and a crumbling faux deer,

the same beast used for target practice,
that one I mistook for flesh and blood.

Spit Shine

The balconies sagged under the weight
of hanging beads and stomping shoes
and before we could jump off the curb
into the surge and shout of new tourists,

a psychic stepped before us, canvas bag
slung round to rest on his hip. He held
his hands up like paddy cakes, and told
me he could guess where I got my shoes.

I tried waving him off, saying I had no
cash to give him, and that the bruises
on my sneakers meant I'd been around,
but he insisted this was on the house.

"You got them shoes right here," he said,
"On Bourbon St." And he kneeled to get
on with the shine while I argued, saying
they'd come across country with me.

The man got through with the first shoe
and said, "Ain't you wearing 'em now?
Then you got 'em right here." I pulled
away when he reached for the second

repeating that I had no money for him,
so he stood, leaving one half of me
with a thick coat of gutter and grime,
then he stowed his polish and brush,

gave a wave and a wink to the lady
clutching my hand, then disappeared
into another bulge of the same crowd
we had wanted to lose ourselves in.

Cheap Cigarettes

Back then,
when all you needed
to get across the border
was lighter skin
and a vague idea
of your home address,
I'd smoke unregulated Marlboros
and drink tequila
from plastic shot glasses
and felt like life was as simple
as reset buttons
or the to-be-continued pages
of comic books,
and I'd fill my pockets
with knives and brass knuckles
and prescriptions that my father
just couldn't afford to buy in the states,
then pass children on my way home,
sitting on bridges over clogged streets
and rivers of sewage,
shaking my head
when they tried to sell me tiny
packages of chicle,
or handmade figurines
because I'd spent all I had
on what was more
important.

The Content is Irrelevant

Our first night in Hawaii, my mother
couldn't sleep, her brain turning over
and over with the notion that her only child,
a three-year-old, would find the strength
to climb up or between the iron railing
and float down the seven stories
to the still, chlorinated hotel pool.

Our last night on cruise ship Freedom,
I laid awake, my mind shifting through
the scenarios of my mother's death
at the hands of some exotic virus
she'd picked up in Jamaica or the Caymans,
and how I'd find the strength to climb up
or over the walls of my future without her.

They call this obsessive thinking, the pros,
akin to flipping on a light switch a dozen
times, or scrubbing your hands until they bleed,
and along with a lineage stretching
back to the Carpathian mountains, I'll share
this, forever, with my mother, and my children,
like a tic or an unearthed secret.

> The whispered insistence of love,
> of family—our durable bond found
> in the jagged peaks and valleys of maybe,
> of possibly,
> of what if.

Security Deposit

We called him the Fledgling,
a recent broken home dropout
who needed a place to unroll
his frayed sleeping bag, so
come the first of the September,
we cleaned out the spare room,
my girl and I, then watched
as he hung posters, and settled in,
making himself comfortable first
with our friends, the spread
in the fridge, and the lion's share
of the white drugs I was selling
out the back door, then moving
up to the paring knife he used
on his wrists to spray a Pollack
imitation across the wallpaper,
and the long, bumpy ambulance
ride we called for him, all before
he could give us a cent for rent,
so we left his room how it was,
not vacuuming or boxing up,
or bothering to clean the walls
when we decided to move out.

Lockdown

Before the sound of fireworks, a student said,
"I just didn't have the time to finish."
And I tried to lecture over the the first
pops of the firecracker, thinking:
How could it be July already?

A lesson plan replaced by the language
of tennis shoes and heels slapping the polished tile.
Then doors began to slam, one after another,
thump, thump, thump,
like a ship taking on water—all hands
sealing their passages from the torrent.

My father told me his school had drills during
the missile crisis. They had to get
beneath wooden desks and lace their fingers
to protect their skulls from the coming blast,
a proper helmet against fiery debris.

And after I closed my doors, the desk against one,
my back against the other,
I demanded students do the same,
as if the scratched oak tops could stand
in opposition of lead, of focused hate,
of a rambling manifesto.

Then came the ringing in our ears,
the scent of a struck match,
the hashtags for change,
the candlelight vigils,
the presidential address,
the earnest promises,
the slowed trickle of information,
the changed channel,
the next story.

And the next.
And the next.

Still, the roll sheet is light one name,
someone who'll never find the time to finish.

Time to Buzz the Tower, Goose

Somewhere outside of Da Trang,
or was it Hue?
My father's helicopter was shot down.
He'd walked out of the wreck alone, his only scars
still, were those from the hazing of hot bullet casings
delivered from the the 50cal barrel to his open collar.
And before the crash, he'd been sure to give them too.

About twenty miles outside of Riverside,
or was it San Bernardino?
My father took his motorcycle the long way around.
In the fast lane, he took a minute to watch the sun melt
into the earth, the image replaced by brake lights
and collapsed lungs and strung casts like puppetry.
And a son blending into bleached sheets of photographs.

At the corner of Driftwood and Bay,
or was it Cedar?
My father set out on the scooter for milk and whatever else.
The neighborhood mailman was out sick and his fill-in,
distracted by life or some song cutting through the radio,
left my father and the pink Vespa in pieces by the stop sign.
And the red flags stood tall along the rest of his route.

Maybe it was after I got sober,
or was I drinking again?
My father tried to bridge the gap between us.
We pulled out warped pool cues and rolled them over
scratched felt, and we threw on Top Gun, listening
for the familiar soundtrack of Vietnam's jungles.
And thought of how close we'd come to never being able to.

Gunbearer

they come year-round, in herds,
in packs like the wild game
they've studied and pined after
and plan to leave broken, free of flesh,
split wide open like their own
mouths after the gunshots.

I've watched them all die, some
from the first bullet—others, bigger,
more agile creatures like buffalo
or lions take wounds like merit badges
and crawl off to die alone,
somewhere in the trusted brush.

these adventurers, these aliens,
they shout and shake hands, they fire
from the safety of diesel and steel,
looking only to us, perched upon
corrugated bumpers, for full canteens,
or to go out and fetch their new rugs.

the flies beat us to the bodies,
on open eyes and along ragged holes,
and as we draw long knives, some-
times the beast groans, pleads,
to sink, along with their tracks,
into the wet earth, and we allow them.

in camp, hunters drape themselves
with mosquito nets, drink champagne
because the sun has set, while we
sleep outside, beyond the canvas flaps,
listening for the approach of heavy paws,
the roar of tomorrow's prize.

Boys Will Be Boys

Beneath the sag of the top bunk,
she touched me for the first time.

I'd come over for a movie on her
tiny set, but it wasn't long before

we turned from sheen of the teeth
on Leatherface's saw, to those

on our zippers. I remember asking
if she was sure about this, really,

not only for her honor but for mine.
I'd heard the laughs from the locker

room choir, the well-timed jokes
about my uncut skin and difference,

and as I stretched out on her star-burst
sheets—each one rumpled and knotted

and eager—I heard them all again,
replaying while she did her best

to ease my spun mind. To repay her,
I didn't see her again, not even once,

though a few months later, I heard
she was given the right combination

of pills at a party, and had both
her nipples bitten off, and I can't help

but think that same line of snapping
towels left her with their old jokes

and traded satisfied high fives
while gnashing their polished teeth.

That Street with all the Food Carts

Thick pollen in the air, mixing
with the Clorox scent of those cum
trees. Walking downtown, put upon
by the few days of city sun,
our ankles were even thicker,
jutting up from our low top Cons.
Camo shorts and Hatebreed
shirts cut to the shoulders.

We were bad.
We were hardcore.
Thinking we owned the city.

A Jeep, red or black—the color doesn't matter.
Stopped at the nearest light, the driver
laid on the horn and called us faggots.
Andy asked if I wanted to fight.
We tossed up our arms like villagers
with torches and crashed into group of muscles
and old money that slithered across the street.

Head against the base of the closest tree,
the driver pleaded for us to stop,
until the door of Greek Cusina opened,
the chef wedging between us.
Andy and I limped away, hobbling
to the train; knuckles, lips split, and our skin
was stained, red or black—the color doesn't matter.

Nor did it matter that this man
was the only gay friend I had,
and knowing he just received a positive result,
or wondering if I had fought for him,
or for myself. What did matter, was that I couldn't
know for sure whose blood was whose,
or how someone gets HIV.

Or how to see myself after I shied away
from him once we cleaned up. The mixture
of fear and cowardice and shame,
like bloodstains and paint jobs,
kept him at arm's length—
as far as the distance between
those unexplored crevices of sexuality.

And my ignorance of it all.

All my love and thanks to—

Jen and Bruce, my moms and pops, who never once cringed when their son told them he wanted to be a writer / Krista Marie and her unfailing belief in me, the steady whisper before bed and every morning that's helped me to do the same / Susan Reese, who insisted I keep at it, even if it felt like my fingers were crumbling with every letter / John McNally whose support has gotten me through more than just writing. And for getting me completely addicted to vinyl / Daniel Smith, Dayana Stetco, and Skip Fox whose writing workshops and friendships made me feel like it was okay to try anything, and to keep going / Miles & Amy, who continue to show me how to be a real human being / Bray for being "halfen locked" / Kyle (BK Hands) for all the rides home / Matty Grif and Raym-Dawg for struttin' dat ass / Michelle for being the best sister I never had / Seaman Schauer for the chainsaw / Eamonn for being so big / All my friends and sneaker waves at Pacific / My PhD cohort down in Mardi Gras Land / Jackson, the Border Collie with half a face that taught me everything I ever needed to know about unconditional love and loss with the same furry life / And everyone else I'm forgetting while rushing to finish this: I couldn't have done it without you, and I swear I'll buy you a drink next time I see you.

Cover Photo: "Memories of the Body Part II" by Susan David, an interdisciplinary artist based in Lafayette, Louisiana. Her creations, influenced by the symbolic nature of water, play with her theories concerning early natural biology, memory, identity, themes of violence and destruction, in connection with the human form.

Drew Attana was born on a now defunct Air Force base east of Los Angeles, then spent the better part of twenty years kicking around the West Coast, getting into trouble from Tijuana to Portland. After getting his act together, Drew studied English at Portland State, received his MFA from Pacific University, and in 2014, began working on his PhD in Creative Writing at the University of Louisiana at Lafayette.

When he isn't writing, Drew splits his time between teaching and feeding his debilitating addiction to collecting vinyl. His work has appeared in *Gulf Stream Literary Magazine, Phoebe Literary Journal, Common Ground Review, West Trade Review, Shark Reef Literary Magazine, Merrimack Review* and *Cargo Literary Journal*, among others. Visit him online at drewattana.com.

...and really, he wasn't kidding—if you have any old records collecting dust in an attic, or molding in a basement, send them right over. He'll take 'em.

www.ingramcontent.com/pod-product-compliance
Lightning Source LLC
LaVergne TN
LVHW041522070426
835507LV00012B/1762